The Deputation of Folly

william frank

Copyright © 2025 by William Frank
for Tuckford Bunny Press, a Private Press

TUCKFORD BUNNY PRESS

All rights reserved. Except as permitted under the U.S. Copyright Act of 1976, no part of this publication may be reproduced, distributed or transmitted in any form or by any means, or stored in a database or retrieval system, without the prior written permission of the author.

ISBN-13: 979-8-9877824-5-3

Printed in the United States of America.
First Printing: January 14, 2025

Other books by William Frank:

Novel:
The Grave Listeners (2023)

Poetry:
The Shithouse Trouble of Irv Fugman, Deceased (2022)
The Fulgent Requiem (2021)
Slumgullion (2019)
The Purgatory Elm (2018)
Yuneko (2015)
Fiasco Galante (2014)
The Encolpia (2011)
The Morphine Fawn (2009)

All Tuckford Bunny books are available at Amazon.com and other retailers.

About Tuckford Bunny Press
Tuckford Bunny Press is a private, make-believe Press that publishes the literary works of William Frank. It is the only make-believe company that will publish such funny-headed little books.

Acknowledgements

Floral designs on the Book's back cover and Title page used from the Permission-Free Designs in the book <u>Art Nouveau Motifs</u>, Dover Publications, Inc, Mineola, New York, 2002.

The horned Grotesques on the interior pages of the book are used from the Permission-Free Designs in the book <u>Mythological & Fantastic Creatures</u>, Dover Publications, Inc, Mineola, New York, 2002.

The cover of the book was created using an image from the Permission-Free Designs in the book <u>Frames & Borders Vector Designs</u>, Dover Publications, Inc, Mineola, New York, 2011. The Clouds set behind the image are from a photo taken by the author in the parking lot of the train station in Greenlawn, New York in another one of his dazed lunch break perambulations.

About the Author:

William Frank, an author of eight previous books of poetry and one heartwarming novel, is a man with an amiable façade, a witless disregard for reasonable care and a personal nimbus almost nine feet high. His work has previously appeared in the now-defunct *The Dillydoun Review* (which Tuckford Bunny Press is almost somewhat reasonably sure he didn't personally defunct), the 2022 and 2023 Bards Annual, Rhyme and Punishment, and he was a runner-up for the 2008 *Discovery/The Boston Review* prize offered by the 92nd Street Y.

When not writing, he enjoys long hours of losing at chess, bingeing on Japanese Cinema of the 40's, 50's and 60's, summering with the Devil, punching cryptids in the face and Kulning.

Contents

The Lilies of the Field	1
Tony Island, Professional Cuddler	2
The Death of the Longevity Expert	3
The Fabulous Birthday of Chip Briskley	4
The Flying Saloon of Dick Fungaard	5
Finale at Suds and Spuds	6
Nude on a Crane	7
Vernon Crisp, ex-Pomologist	8
The Quilting Club of St. Theodina Paragon, Heart of Mercy	9
First Watch in the Wards of Moloch	10
Dr. Ingie Potts, Professor of Human Nature	11
A Neck Brace for Myrna and Mumford	12
The Roses of the Hour and the Minute	13
Night Game at the Kubla	14
The Institute for Better Human Affairs Through Science	15
The Numinous Future of Autonomous Delights	16
Poustinia at Harvest Jumbo	17
The Crumbled Little Conclusion of Niv and Pinky	18
USA Eukonkanto Federation vs Doug Fanfare	19
Second Watch in the Wards of Moloch	20
The Coroner in Sunlight	21
The Dappled Cielo of Flightless Birds	22
The Many Dazzling Facets of Terry Gales	23
Astoundment of a Thousand Crias	24
Intermission at The Garden Musical of the Saints	25
The Folly of Folly Paperwork	26
The Cancellation of Recess at Bumblebee Elementary	27
The Jigsaw Passions of National Puzzlers	28
The Corkscrew Graces of Our Lonely Dives	29
Confused Imbecile Cryptid Mêlée and Rapine	30

Fred Crompton, Pet Psychologist	31
The Scrutable Disasters of Faith and Work	32
Third Watch in the Wards of Moloch	33
The Temptation Officer	34
The Empire Winter Spectacular	35
Froid Unlimited: The Comfort of Care	36
Juniper Billows, Disinformation Expert	37
Decollation at The Ladies Life Group's Backyard Pā'ina	38
The Happy Rainbow Nuclear Disaster	39
When the Night is Now, You Need Milgrew Man Control…	40
Bale and Beauty By All Human Lights	41
Uzzo	42
The Eidolon Awards: A Celebration of Deuteragonists	43
The Orchidescent Cyclone of Flaming Chaos	44
Tragōidía at Orcus Bottoms Efficiency Apartments	45
A Company on Upward Dreams	46
Bigfoot Science of St. Paul	47
Fourth Watch in the Wards of Moloch	48
The Little Brown Dog of Dick Fungaard	49
Ballade of an Agelast	50

God hath choosed the Foolish to shame the wise

~ 1 Corinthians 1:27

The Lilies of the Field

At the back of Heaven, in the seedy part of town,
   where the steel mill's closed and the dole line wends
   around Soffy's bar, where the bus line ends,
the Ferris Wheel's lonely, the Fountain's broke down,

in a second-floor office above Chulie's Tamales,
   a staff works with industrial cupidity
   on a vast caseload of earthly stupidity
in the Deputation Office of Human Follies.

The world is helplessly sad and funny
with needs and dreams, for sex and money,
   it burns and tumbles, towers and twirls.

On Parcae machines, working tired and late,
they manage foibles, flops, fantods and Fate:
   behold the Lilies, the big, dumb churls.

Tony Island, Professional Cuddler

Of course, there's no certification program for cuddling
    and so a lot of this is done by intimation and feel,
      just two bodies folded together like harbor seals
whose nipples can chafe in like-minded muddling,

complicated sometimes by the very human fact
    that one of us may have, as of late,
      put on a little semi-professional weight
which can contribute to either party throwing out their back

when trying out some advanced cuddling techniques
    like the Hong Kong Noodle or the Flying Anus,
so while I'm not insensitive to your horrible injuries,

Sloane, I still must take exception to the critique
    you posted on my site that I was *"amorphous and heinous"*
just because you were strangled purple inadvertently.

The Death of the Longevity Expert

The Springtime Super Half-Off Event at Rexby Mall,
   bristling with balloons, unicycles, costumes and clowns,
   with the biggest, most dazzling deals in town
was nearly spoiled by thirty-four-year-old Marcel-Fred St. Paul

who was bisected in the spirit of the Sale, and keelhauled,
   circling the escalator round and round
   after an Oompah Band knocked him down,
caught his head in a tuba and trampled his balls.

His top half was catapulted into the petting zoo
   while his legs and part of his ass were flung
into the screaming nubiles of Forever 21

despite St. Paul's strict sleep and barbell regimen,
   his berry diet, soft orgasm program,
and spiritual belief in his trust fund, true love and jiu jitsu.

The Fabulous Birthday of Chip Briskley

It was Chip's stupid birthday at Magic Gene's Playground
    until forty-one-year-old Lester Lane Levine
    somehow got trapped in the claw machine
at five foot one and three hundred pounds.

Upside-down, face smooshed against the glass
    and covered in stuffed animals, children played the game
    as he kicked and cursed til the fire department came
to effect a rescue and pull the claw from his ass.

It was an operation even Faith knew was doomed:
Breaking the glass could get shards in his eyes
    and pulling him through the chute only wedged his fat

so they pulled the top off, buttered his sides and tried
sucking him out using a high-powered vacuum
    which tangled his legs around his head, and he shat.

The Flying Saloon of Dick Fungaard

While I can and cannot explain why my car is in the house
   and this poor family is dead with stunned expressions
   in a scene that looks vaguely like depraved aggression
and only the cat to ferment with meows

it is my particular regret and personal feeling
   that the lack of curbs out front was a contributor
   that could have stopped me blasting through the door
though I'm to blame for the tire marks on the ceiling

and perhaps it happened just like the police complaint
   and one or two things went especially wrong,
I may not fit the definition of a saint,
   beauty proves too much and vice too strong,
but all I need is a new coat of paint
   and God's great mercy to help me get along.

Finale at Suds and Spuds
(Lentil County's Original French Fry Shop and Laundromat Since 1982)

There's a time when a fool's life becomes
   untwisted from any savor or anticipation.
   The heart dulls in its longing caffeination
and no longer eats its cake down to the crumbs.

The Lyrebird Cafe by the lone esplanade
   closes in Heaven's half hour of silence.
   I leave a tip of eight dollars and sixteen cents
which is everything in my pocket that I had.

Jolly was on the corner making balloon animals
   and twisting together Crumbles, his cat,
who followed him home one day from a carnival

when, during a fold, the balloon just popped
   which sounded like a gun to a nearby cop
who shot him nineteen times into a laundromat.

Nude on a Crane

Carol Venison circled upside-down in a swirling wind
 as the crane pulled her from the rubble that was Toxley Hall
  after paragliding through a billboard, crashing through its wall
and folding a support beam, collapsing it, and she was pinned.

With her breasts knotted around her head, she thought
 about all that has and hasn't happened to her
  since the divorce, vaguely wondering where her clothes were,
and gloomed about causing another public onslaught.

Risking her life to feel alive at aged forty-eight
 seemed like a good idea until that first loop de loop
caused her to shit her pants and hallucinate,

she veered into town, ripped down high-tension wires,
 exploded through Toxley Hall spread-eagle and on fire
killing, among others, a Gliding Survivors Support Group.

Vernon Crisp, ex-Pomologist

What a beautiful rolling apple orchard
   Vernon Crisp dressed each day for his wife,
   Gorgón Quinsy-Crisp, the love of his life,
who preferred the pippins of her lover, Richard,

a drunk with two lazy eyes and unemployed.
   But it was after the *Heirloom Apple Show* in Quebec
   when Vernon found Dick's underwear in a peck
that it all went feral and got destroyed.

This kind fruit scientist, sweet, semi-Catholic, relaxed,
went balls off his perch and pulled down his axe
   and, after enjoying the lift of a Pomme d'Api,

raged through the orchard chopping everything down
until the one with his wife and Dick in the crown
   fell forward with their weight, crushing him with the tree.

The Quilting Club of St. Theodina Paragon, Heart of Mercy

Let's start a quilt for which we can all be proud
   after all that nonsense that happened last Tuesday
   and really showcase our needle turn appliqué
while using some fun jelly rolls to make a shroud

for Judy, that insufferable, guzzling bitch
   before she returns from her trip to Saint-Tropez
   and tells us all again the *proper* way
to be an asshole about every little stitch.

Unfortunately, the shroud was too chubby and too short
so they beat up her fawning friend Brenda for sport,
   with her own walker, and then she was smothered.

Judy was simply set on fire with a propane torch
and what was left shoved under Mildred's porch
   which led to the state's largest one day arrest of grandmothers.

First Watch in the Wards of Moloch

All I have left in this world is my favorite sweater
   you bought that makes me look like an old satyr
   and a picture of us I keep by my desk on the radiator
where I'm biting you like a playful Gordon Setter,

trying to write an elegy, pastoral or even a love letter
   defiant, kind, sensible, in the face of all sabres,
   this land of Nightfall ravenous, dogs and dictators,
from the folly of Life where we never know better.

At the same time nothing makes sense, it is all too familiar:
excess yet poverty; pride and stupidity; lunacy and war;
   the simultaneity of good with all that's bad.

We can never stray too false or too far
from where the center of the human heart
   loves with its whole fire and goes mad.

Dr. Ingie Potts, Professor of Human Nature
(*Lectures on Anonymity, Atavism and Animal Pleasure
as Activating Agents of the Human Abyss*)

Human behavior is always in a headlong downslope
   into its roiling pit of lust and selfish abjection
    (if one wants to call it the Id, I have no objection)
though we've had no past way to measure its depth and scope

until the modern-day invention of its electron microscope
   that can see Human Nature's elemental oubliette,
   that microscope, of course, being the Internet,
and now we know all humans, at base, are feral, rancid dopes.

My mother fell from a helicopter tour at nine hundred feet
with her Cane Corso into a puppet show on the street
   which generated spoofs, memes and ten billion views.

When something terrible happens to someone you love or you,
it's a tragedy. But in Human Nature's exuberant derangement,
   when it happens to someone else, it's entertainment.

A Neck Brace for Myrna and Mumford

Mum Ruffins was in a conflagratory emotional spiral
   and so reached out to his Life Coach double-quick
    for even the vanity of crying hysterically in public
felt flat, despite the brave episode going viral

but Myrna was trying to effect her own heroic catharsis
   after another bad date who looked nothing like his photo,
    lied about having a job, a house, being a commando
and probably had a micropenis. *People fall on their arses*

was all she could muster since this wasn't about her
which, if either of them would stop to consider
   this little cosmic capsule of commonsense,

they might actually learn how to live alone and well
and Mumford wouldn't have crashed his Toyota Tercel
   through her kitchen, shed and brand-new fence.

The Roses of the Hour and the Minute

I now know the secret of Life and Death:
   we are, until our appointed day and hour,
   invincible to all catastrophes and powers
but when it's time, we're mush like haroseth.

It's what the death of Baldr shows:
   Impervious to every projectile,
   dames, drink and violence wild,
he was killed at a touch with mistletoe.

Phil Litz, dreamy, flush, avuncular,
who liked crosswords, cats and going out at dawn
   to soak up every bit of the glorious outside

tangled in his robe and tumbled down the lawn
where he fell on a sprinkler head and cut his jugular
   bleeding out in his underwear until he died.

Night Game at the Kubla

It was the playoffs at the sprawling Kubla Cola Sports Complex
    between the May Day Miners and Carson City Pioneers,
    the first series for either team in seventy-six years,
at four thousand dollars a ticket, even in the upper decks,

with May Day down two scores with forty-five minutes gone,
    their best player ejected and things looking woeful
    it was then Matt Glistens decided to make his proposal
to Anne Treats on the Jumbotron.

Anne vomited. She was going to break up with Matt
right after the playoffs, during drinks at Shootables,
    but only because he had spent so much on the game

otherwise, she would have told him at his mother's funeral.
Before she could decline, he slipped in her sick & hydroplaned
    from the nosebleeds to the field with a splat.

The Institute for Better Human Affairs Through Science

The Institute for Better Human Affairs Through Science
   was in court this week after CloudNews broke the story
   of sex, murder and corruption at a laboratory
that produced occult data and dangerous public guidance

citing, for example, a grossly irresponsible study
   asserting that those who like to consume shumai
   were twelve times more likely to die
in a tandem parachuting accident with a lover or buddy

after an investigation by the Skydiving Association revealed
   those conclusions lacked scientific rigor and experiment
   but were clearly just manifested wish fulfillment
by a Research lead whose shumai-loving wife, Camille,

was sleeping with colleague and best man Throb Steele,
both found wrapped in a parachute at an airfield.

The Numinous Future of Autonomous Delights

As sober a man you'll ever find, that Thurman Aloysius,
   circumspect and prudent in every practical way,
   something of an agelast, I've heard people say,
but nonetheless firm, principled and judicious

so that when you met him in the shops
   or in the Plum garden, you felt right away
   that you were as wicked as lingerie,
your toes like little wedges in an icebox

and so imagine our shock and horror
(and great relief) when we found out
   that he was hit by a self-driving car

as it whipped out of the West Side roundabout
and he was dragged into Ann Taylor Loft
   right through the bras as his cock was torn off.

Poustinia at Harvest Jumbo
For where your treasure is, there your heart will be also.
(Luke 12:34)

There was blood, hair and teeth all over the parking lot.
  It started with two guys cursing and shoving each other
  then bloomed into friends, girlfriends, one guy's mother
blasting each other in the face over a parking spot

because they're all too stupid, fat and lazy
  to park forty feet from the store and walk.
  One guy ruptured a testicle. Mom went down with a squawk.
Of course, I watched. It was too good crazy.

Life can be so peccant and conniving, too droll to understand,
   funny at every expense and pointless with despair
while wasting like a nobody on line at the register

until I saw a nine-year-old girl holding the hand
  of her worshipful five-year-old sister
with vigilant assurance, such innocence of care.

The Crumbled Little Conclusion of Niv and Pinky

Niv Kipley was divorced so he took up joggling,
   and managed with practice, zeal and a little natural flair
   to run a six-minute mile with five balls in the air,
getting a misplaced lift from everyone goggling

at his dexterity, colorful kit and mind-boggling
   disregard for dignity or reasonable care
   until he fell over his balls down the stairs
at Beso Beach helplessly ogling

the beach bunnies terraforming a seaside Paradise.
He broke his arm in two places and, concussed,
   was rammed head on by a city bus

as he wandered without his shorts into the street
landing in a heap at his ex-wife's feet
   with her new triathlete boyfriend, Bryce.

USA Eukonkanto Federation vs Doug Fanfare
*Lentil County Courthouse, 4th Judicial District,
on behalf of the Federation and its Co-Founders
Mr. and Mrs. Lawrence and Claire "Sidecar" Tutters*

It was Doug's third disgraceful arrest
   (and fourth police beating) in as many weeks
   for property damage, disturbing the peace,
grievous bodily harm, arson and civil unrest

and leaving his latest six-hour inquest,
   (where he had to dramatically reenact how he set fire
   to the Opera house, trapping the Fireman's Choir)
upset and distracted, he crashed into a wife-carrying contest

tangling on the husband's shoulders where he was carried
as a threesome (though Doug wasn't especially married
in the sacred and civil sense to Larry *or* Claire)

causing them to drift off course and down a hill
where Doug and the wife had a torrid affair
until he ejaculated, they tumbled and the couple was killed.

Second Watch in the Wards of Moloch

The shops are busy and the bars pack them in
   with music, Appletinis, the lusts of Sabbats.
   In plays, frolics, restaurants, the town's forgot
the enemies without and within.

Food trucks, sports and open malls
   are the outward signs of our liberty
   while the spires of celebrity
loom with aspirations over all.

The wolves are coming for the same impassioned few
lost in every notion of the goodness of humankind
   who, for our worth, potential and justice, resist.

We worship power, strength and beauty, despite their truth,
and have faith in our joy. Lush the Sazerac with orange twist
   with matching watchband that mimics an orange rind.

The Coroner in Sunlight

It was a somewhat somber Grand Opening at Headspace,
   the new Burger Shop and Thai Chicken Cafe,
   because of a massacre earlier in the day
when the now ex-Manager snapped and shot up the place.

How many times do we have to suffer this National disgrace?!
   cried Ted Lickey, refilling an iced tea and waving his gun.
   Though the crowd concurred, it panicked everyone
so they drew their rifles and shot each other in the face

while enjoying the two-dollar Chicken bucket and cornbread,
   blowing out the windows and the french fry machine,
   a whole clip going through Lickey's balls and spleen,
hitting a table of grandmothers behind him in their heads

who spun firing into the new Manager, Pauline,
who enfiladed a service dog and covey of teens.

The Dappled Cielo of Flightless Birds

After his Acorn Stairlift shot him through his attic
   at speeds of 450 miles per hour
   landing him atop the town's water tower
Rez Polly's behavior became especially erratic,

wearing morning and night only a sheened tuxedo,
   adopting an escalating series of lifestyle prohibitions,
   hating comedy, music, babies and nutrition
as expected after being a human torpedo

until he fell in love with a woman who taught him to trust,
to see life in all its possibilities and opened his heart,
   they traveled, danced, bought a house at the shore,

indulged her love of kites, cookies and go-carts
til she was shot from their Stairlift through a fireworks store
   where babies watched her smash the aisles and combust.

The Many Dazzling Facets of Terry Gales

Terry's life was a series of tramplings, mockeries and rejections
   but he always maintained an unshakeable optimism
   in the human spirit's resilience, goodness and dynamism,
seeing the vagaries of life as a foundation of its perfection.

In the interests of sparing others from mistakes,
   he secured a plum contract to write a book
   for Tuckford Bunny Press called, *The Burning Look:
How to Tell If Your Eclipse Glasses Are Fake*

but he sadly never realized that aspiration:
while doing research ahead of the eclipse,
   staring extensively into the sun, he went blind,

sterile, daft and burned off his lips
then wandered through an abandoned army installation
   where he was blown to Chiclets by an unaccounted mine.

Astoundment of a Thousand Crias

How sad and often things go awry.
   How troublesome is life, how dearly we have to pay,
   inventing the act of wishing because nothing goes our way,
the romantic expectation in a lie.

Life is astonishing. The snow swirls
   upside-down and in between
   graveside roses like Torvill and Dean
while we make little confrontations with the world.

I came home late bedraggled by a Doom.
   I wandered by the sea. I closed out the bar.
   I then tore the door off my neighbor's car

   parallel parking and set off its alarm
   which riled the next-door Alpaca farm
and they trampled him to death in his living room.

Intermission at The Garden Musical of the Saints

All in Heaven is ordered, kind and rational
   because of Love, and each adores the other's Grace.
   The Great Mourning constrains and makes chaste
what is despotic in every soul in Hell.

Only the earth is insane and cursed
   with our mind, our power, our liberty.
   Our Natures devour us bitterly.
Great is our divinity, onward the perverse.

Hope has its admirers, and Mercy its claims,
They deserve Their Faith and popular esteem
   but Misery is perfect: It knows Its aims

and has no impediments. It needs no elaborate schemes
but simply pulls a thread or snuffs a flame
   to consume all Love can do because Love dreams.

The Folly of Folly Paperwork

Hello Sir, Most Illustrious, how are you?
   It's Heaven, I'm fine. What is it?
   You've had such a glow lately, I thought I'd visit.
Claremont! Do you remember case number 116411741155782?

*Duane Marbles, God's belovéd, so of course
   exempted from Deputation, what about him?*
   There may have been a slight twitch in the algorithm.
Twitch. Slight twitch. With remorse.

Claremont, I promise you, I'm in no mood today.
I'm as upset as you are, really, if I could I'd quit.
What the Hell happened to him?!

He wasn't assigned a Premium Package, I'm glad to say,
he was just… involved… in a soft, very brief hemoclysm
now he's here fingering everyone, cursing and covered in shit.

The Cancellation of Recess at Bumblebee Elementary

I celebrate the human intellect, our spirit of innovation,
   the bold and fearless daring that we do,
   every great achievement and breakthrough
that solves a dire need and improves our station,

advances in medicine, astronomy, automation,
   colliders, machine learning, prostheses
   to solve ourselves the questions of theodicy
but Fate has its own inventions and navigation.

Bob Peplow, a delivery person for Pizza Taj Mahal,
was eating a slice of the customer's order when his GPS,
recalibrating, directed him to make three quick lefts

until he crashed through the Sunshine Execution Center wall
next to the kindergarten where he interrupted a firing squad
and, covered in pepperoni, gave his soul to God.

The Jigsaw Passions of National Puzzlers

Life itself is a puzzle of confounding Grace
   so I live a quiet, faraway life alone
   with my goldfish, hummels and slide trombone
and a small library with a long bookcase

shelved with puzzles rather than books.
   I enjoy five-thousand-piece afternoons
   of seascapes, bazaars, wildlife, balloons,
famous cities and out of the way brooks

and I think I'm pretty good at it, too.
   So when the National Speed Puzzling Competition
came to our state, I traveled four hours by canoe

to the Holiday Inn, if not to win, then at least to place
   when this jerk had some sort of nocturnal emission,
knocking my pieces to the floor. I shot him in the face.

The Corkscrew Graces of Our Lonely Dives

Theosis Jones was Diving Nationals' rising star,
   chiseled, golden, beautiful and tall
   who hit the water without a splash at all
and emerged with a nimbus like Roman Mars

and for the Lentil County competition planned
   a special move whose elegant twists and twirls
   would defy physics and faith ahead of Worlds
held in Fukuoka, Japan.

However, his muscular gifts and the tension of the board
shot him into the roof where he was pinned and gored
   and they evacuated the arena to effect a rescue

so no one saw the dive he called the Firebrand
falling from the roof, with its grace and derring-do,
   albeit into the Concession stand.

Confused Imbecile Cryptid Mêlée and Rapine

Oliver Rumbly-Sprain had always loved the outdoors
   despite being abandoned as an ugly child
   in a National Park and growing up in the wild,
responsible for the Sasquatch sightings of local lore

and hunted endlessly by Bigfoot Science of St. Paul.
   In order to survive, he became one with Nature
   and modelled his life after all its creatures
caring for them, hunting with them, communicating with calls

so when the EC Gull Screeching Competition came
to the Park Convention Center's Buskin Room
   Oliver crashed through the doors when he heard

what sounded like the distress of a thousand birds
being strangled, humiliated, raped and maimed.
   He repaid the guests in kind, sparing only those in costume.

Fred Crompton, Pet Psychologist

After his last dachshund committed suicide
   wrestling with body dysmorphia and phobias of separation,
   Fred decided on a different approach with this Dalmatian
whose detached Humping Disorder left the public terrified.

Coping behaviors consisted of biting, drug use and prostitution
   in both the dog and the owner, a respected
   pastor at the Church of the Resurrected
who begged Fred, nude and in tears, for solutions.

Fred decided to try a session of Regression therapy,
taking Waffles back to when he was a puppy
   when, in a state of deep hypnosis, he remembered

being called Fred by a previous owner, with house-training
that left him out all night while it was raining
   and he had a shithouse break. Fred was sexually dismembered.

The Scrutable Disasters of Faith and Work

Sayville Sawler was a drudge for Serenity, Inc.
   working there as middle manager for twenty-six years,
   divorced, living in a motel, desperately in arrears,
whose company was catastrophically on the brink.

The office had become a blazing pressure-cooker
   whose executives raided the only refuge he's known
   while demanding he fix the problems right now and alone
while the Owner's in his office farting on a hooker.

As the stock price tumbled to ninety-seven cents,
the CFO was upstairs shredding documents,
   the top guys were arrested and they filed for bankruptcy.

On the last day at the office, his life in a box,
Sayville slumped down to the Bergamot docks
   to mourn with an ice cream by the sea.

Third Watch in the Wards of Moloch

The bars close, the Wards are drunk and fed
   and the streets clear. At home on their devices,
   they upload a photo, consume their last vices,
text their hieroglyphics and finally go to bed.

Some linger. Prostitutes on a 'date'
   disappear in cars. The homeless cannot vanish
   while runaways and drug fiends rove around famished.
Some make it to dawn. For most, it's far too late.

Sleeping on a bench with a book over his face
about weddings, or the Cynical Genius Illusion,
   that never quite shields his eyes

from the lights of Orange Theory or Cupcake Fusion,
this is the squalid liberty and human disgrace
   of the eternal palace, its jewels of hope and lies.

The Temptation Officer

Though not directly under its auspices, we often serve as well
   the Deputation Office to arouse human nature,
   to prick one into Folly or present a human wager
for the entertainment of Heaven or a Judgment of Hell.

What is folly but a hot estrangement
   from conscience, consequences, commonsense
   for which human nature has no defense
in its primal fund of desire and derangement.

Though hardened in our fires to sympathy,
we recognize our kinship and admit the tragedies
   that come to a confused and disgusting animal;

but there are still redemptions, however slight,
and fools can be beloved by God despite
   we are gladly called to be Destroying angels.

The Empire Winter Spectacular

Anticipation was hot all around the room
   at the combined Fashion Show and Tyrant's Ball
   held at the spectacular Pantokratic Hall
for the unveiling of *Anacyclosis*, the new parfum

from the illustrious House of Doryphoros.
   A celebration with a winter theme
   and decadent savor of Ancien Régime,
at the height of the music, ecstasy and excess

the lighting rigs fell from the domes of ice
setting fire to the curtains bathed in citron,
   the gondolas of food, the birds of paradise,

the gartered children, wigged bankers, topless matrons,
all engulfed in flames with hideous screams
   and notes of peppermint, lemon and strawberry cream.

Froid Unlimited: The Comfort of Care

It was Clovis Holmes' first day in International purchasing
   and he was tasked with shipping from our vendor in Perth
   thirty industrial refrigeration units worth
five hundred thousand dollars to our warehouse in Lansing

but both parties struggled on the call with their respective accents
   and instead of placing an order for thirty units
   misheard, and confirmed, thirty Eunuchs
to be bundled in the crates with the pressure relief vents.

Finding thirty Eunuchs in modern-day Australia
was surprisingly difficult and the outlays required
   for procurement, alcohol, removal of genitalia

resulted in massive delays and cost overruns,
protests from Human Rights organizations
   and a crippling PR nightmare. Both men were fired.

Juniper Billows, Disinformation Expert

June could see in the Christmas Card the tell-tale signs
   from a mother-in-law who believed alien abductions
   were part of a Zionist plot to force liposuctions
on unbaptized babies to consign

them to the Hell of Everything Wrong with the World:
   To her grandchildren and daughter, she sent love and prayers
   then went off about Food Chemists who implant unawares
men like June who then fuck animals and underage girls.

June dropped the family off at their grandmother's
then went to the store to get eggnog, pastries and cashews,
grumbling about another bonkers holiday,

when his car skidded on some ice down the highway
which plowed him through an orphanage and a petting zoo
where he blew a goat and orphans were face-smothered.

Decollation at The Ladies Life Group's Backyard Pā'ina

The summer neighborhood was lively at every house,
   each family gathered for their own tribal celebration,
   a birthday, anniversary, engagement, graduation
or just a barbecue to eat, drink and carouse

so the LLG, too, a spiritual Coaching organization,
   were having a Trauma/Healing party with a Hawaiian theme
   around fun, food, emotional truth and self-esteem
and circled around Ethel's poi to express their admiration

when there appeared out of the sky screaming and on fire
what looked to them like two boyfriends in anal rapport
but later found to be Tandem Skydivers hired

to land with Roman Candles at the party next door
who overshot the mark executing a back loop Banana
and exploded through the hula, decapitating Hannah.

The Happy Rainbow Nuclear Disaster

Bun Pudluck knew that trouble came in oodles
and being dumpy, sexless, out of touch were factors.
Bring Your Pet to Work Day at the Happy Rainbow Reactor
surrounded by snakes, tarantulas, fish and Labradoodles

who were genetically unhinged and didn't want to be there
was the wrong day to eat lunch at his station
to avoid the breakroom's mocking cachinnations
for looking like Phyllis Diller right down to the hair.

Unwrapping his sandwich set the cold, panting crowd
into a feeding frenzy that took Bun down
under his desk where the mauling ripped the wires

from his board, which then blazed into a fire
and chain reaction that obliterated the town
with a towering blast and doodle-shaped cloud.

When the Night is Now, You Need Milgrew Man Control…

Wendell Cockley was waiting on a three-hour hold
   for Customer Service from Milgrew Man Pomades
   while staving off the cops behind a barricade
in his basement apartment after being sold

an Unregulated Hair Replacement Supplement
   made with monkey agita, biotin and virility peptides
   collected from carnies, which worked as advertised:
it replaced his hair with a fundament

that was pubic, angry and invulnerable
   to haircuts, blowtorches, surgical intervention,
caused unstoppable chimp farting and hardened his skull

so when in despair he shot himself in the head,
   the bullet ricocheted off his helmet and struck Mrs. Benson
right through the neck as she walked her Samoyed.

Bale and Beauty By All Human Lights

Heaven and Hell are against us, and we contend
   with the slavery of our personal stupidity,
   an intellect that merely sharpens our cupidity
with only the passing loves that we can spend.

Our wild desperation forever flourishes,
   how easily we're addicted and ensnared,
   in our hate, greed, humping and despair
we live by the poverty of our wishes.

Why does this man prosper, that child die?
There is joy in life. Things also fall apart.
Death chooses us to fulfill a balance;

we must choose to fulfill a moral balance.
We meet creation and destruction at its size
with only a sad and funny human heart.

Uzzo

Nobody knows how little I am here.
   I seem to make no noise, even when I shout.
   Even good-for-nothing poets no one talks about
squire Giantesses about the town. Me! The Gonfalonier!

Underfoot in the Venetian night like a mink,
   I combed my hair with rosewater.
   I bought a frilled umbrella for Big Alonso's daughter,
my arms overflow with flowers black and pink.

If I brought you a bowl of strawberries, a basket of plums,
would you see me among their succulent sums
   and grant me the honor of a Sunday morning stroll?

But Venus! Dread One! How lonely Sunday comes!
You scatter the mice as I walk home through the slums
   as curtains close above, dogged by Your barcarole!

The Eidolon Awards: A Celebration of Deuteragonists

After years in support, it was finally time to shine a light
   on the sidekick, assistant, canine companion or foil
    for all their steady, reliable sacrifice and toil
in service to the hero on their own Gala Night

moved at the last minute to the Bingo Room and Dinner Hall
   at Ron's Off-Ramp Lodge and Motel in San Bonanza
   after organizers double-booked a competing extravaganza
for the Term Life Sales Association at the luxurious Parsifal.

No one's sure what set things off: the potluck dinner, the corked wine,
lack of parking, general admission seating, the well-meaning sign
"Welcome Second Fiddles: The Real Stars in the Firmament"

combined perhaps with years of envy, unequal pay and resentment
but when Duncan Special asked Buddy Sancho to save him a seat
a brawl erupted that destroyed the Lodge then rioted in the street.

The Orchidescent Cyclone of Flaming Chaos
"We just don't have any resources to support and de-stress our residents after such a cataclysmic tragedy," said Lt. Webb "Big Schlong" Herbfoot during his appeal for help on Thursday.
~The Daily Daiquiri

Mayhem erupted today in the little town of Daiquiri
   when Junior QA Technician Valmont Greene
     somehow got sucked into the Ball Smoosh™ machine
which caused a titanic explosion at the Stress Ball Factory

leveling most of the surrounding Manufacturing District
   and showering Main Street with flaming balls
     that set fire to local shops, the bank and Town Hall,
described by Ball Burn Victim Mud Coffey as 'apocalyptic'.

Trauma Counselors at the scene are struggling to manage
the religious mania and emotional damage,
   the shit terrors, personality splits and despair

with one unfortunate Daiquiri resident, Myrtle Sweet,
completely catatonic and ass-up in the street
   after Valmont's penis landed in her hair.

Tragōidía at Orcus Bottoms Efficiency Apartments

Behold the victim of the gods, Craig Gloeser,
   who, for his boring stories, goat hygiene, misplaced Pride,
   was shot out of Poseidon's Waterslide
across Splash Paradise, over the highway and through the Grocer's

where he destroyed the Produce department on impact.
   O Men of Thebes, and also Hot Beach City,
   there is no escape from the gods' ferocity,
consider Bob's Greek Chorus Service for your next setback!

Craig dashed to his bedsit shedding vegetables and fruit
with a competing Greek Chorus in dogged pursuit
   followed by the police, Channel One News and half the town

where the gods were waiting with all their vengeful powers
to cram Craig and the Chorus into his shower
   where their groins locked, they dogpiled and drowned.

A Company on Upward Dreams

After Froid Unlimited resolved their Human Trafficking case,
    completed mandated Anti-Genital Mutilation training,
    and mounted an advertising campaign reframing
the company as a Eunuch-positive and idiot-free workplace

new International purchasing representative Derek Stropworth
    ordered four thousand Brand Kangaroo Refrigeration Scales
    this time, following a new company policy, via email
from his replacement counterpart, Bossie Quayles, in Perth

a mode any reasonable, modern professional would expect.
    However, overloaded with tasks and working late,
Derek never noticed that the email's autocorrect

changed the order to Contraband Kangaroo Mutilation Males
    who destroyed the office when they exploded from the crates,
attacked the Eunuchs in HR and the girls in Retail.

Bigfoot Science of St. Paul

In hindsight, we wouldn't have expected to see one in the mall
   and I guess he was missing some of the tell-tale Sasquatch signs
   though the odor was there, the fartface, the advanced hairline
that started at the back of his neck and ended past his balls

well, yes, Officer, we could've used some more scientific discretion
   but when this big dumb cryptid put us in a Belgian Headlock
   and started ramming our faces into his dirty Bigfoot cock
after asking a very simple "Are You a Fucking Sasquatch" question

it tells me, Sir, we were very clearly on the right track
and my only regret, beyond the biting & trampling at Shake Shack
   that spilled over into the JC Penney and erupted in gunplay

between us and, of course, the fire and the people that died,
was the fact that we weren't able to take the creature outside
   but we were afraid he would just jump in his car and drive away!

Fourth Watch in the Wards of Moloch

Suffering is eternal. It moves on while we weep.
   A compact of jackals. I'm beyond even *carmen et error*.
   I wake at dawn in the pollution of terror,
the rare night desperate exhaustion grants me sleep.

The despair of martyrs to see future after future.
   Deportations and parades. Eagles and axes.
   The poor without care. The rich without taxes.
There's no salvation beyond violence, sex and lucre.

It is an animal that laughs that is Regent,
a pike driver, an accountant, a wife.
   Moloch is the people; in His virtues, we conspire.

Black hangs the clusters of prosperity. Sorrow is lambent.
Everywhere are the melodies of human life
   and a third of the stars are waiting with our fire.

The Little Brown Dog of Dick Fungaard

Is that dog wearing a scarf?! She screamed
   as Muffins careered in a Ford Fiesta,
   wheels on fire, and drove through Vanessa
paying at the register for Cookie Dough ice cream.

Yes, and it's pink! I yelled
   doing an army crawl across the floor
   as Muffins crushed every part of the store,
sprinkles flying in the explosions of Hell.

I couldn't tell if it was Muffins, Esther-Jean or Arlo
   cursing as the car flipped and melted in the heat
just as the wavy pink scarf got tangled

around Mrs. Briggs-White, who was strangled,
   then whipped out of her bloomers through the window
and bounced on her tits down the street.

Ballade of an Agelast
Vain the joy for which our pain must pay.
~Samuel Johnson, after Horace, Epist. I ii 55

I stumble each morning out of the bordello.
    I go to Irving's Candy Shop each day.
I take the Seven bus back to the depot
    then wander round the wharf like a stray.
    The Leper Colony waves me away,
I ring my bell and they ring back to me
    to thank me for the rum and pink bouquet.
Life is driftless with Fate and wisdom, and these are Folly.

I watch the day's condemned wash the Gallows
    while all the shops put out their Spring displays.
The Scaffold's decorated with orange bows,
    dogs do tricks, balloons flutter, a band plays.
    I order a coffee cake at the café
and then decide I'm not really hungry.
    Down the street, I buy a Pumpkin latte.
Life is driftless with Fate and wisdom, and these are Folly.

What difference does it make where we go?
    Why bother at all wearing a toupee?
Who cares if Time's too fast or too slow,
    it's always the same old thing anyway.
    I guess I should get to the Gallows, yesterday
I was so far in the back, I couldn't see.
    I hope there isn't another rain delay.
Life is driftless with Fate and wisdom, and these are Folly.

Envoi

It's best to keep busy, isn't that what people say?
    Joy may gird your spirit, it all just makes me weary.
And where tragedy's concerned, I prefer the matinée,
    Executions at night are drunk and dreary
and end in fights, fires, dogs and pepper spray.
Life is driftless with Fate and wisdom, and these are Folly.

TUCKFORD BUNNY PRESS

Welcome to the end, and with thanks.

Visit us at www.TuckfordBunnyPress.com for books of every spectacle.

www.ingramcontent.com/pod-product-compliance
Lightning Source LLC
Chambersburg PA
CBHW060857050426
42453CB00008B/1004